THE PURPOSE OF THE CHURCH

By

R. D. FRAZIER

True Apostolic Church Series

Book 1

Truth Tabernacle Publications
18027 San Bernardino Ave.
Bloomington, CA 92316

ISBN: 1530733863

Special Thanks:

I would like to thank Brother Phillip Kelley for all of the guidance, editing and set up help with publishing this book. I owe a great debt of gratitude to you. Also, we are not islands unto ourselves we are not self-made men, I would be remiss to not mention or give thanks to all of the great Apostolic men of God that have influenced my life and helped make me who I am. I would be afraid if I started naming them to miss even one, but suffice it to say there were many, some have gone on to be with the Lord and some continue to be great Elders among us.

Thank you,

Elder R.D. Frazier

Foreword:

I want to start by saying that I deeply appreciate this book by Bro. Frazier. As I read it, I thought of the scripture in Philippians 2:5, "Let this mind be in you, which was also in Christ Jesus." This is the mind of Christ. The scripture teaches us that Jesus came to seek and to save the lost. As of this month, June 2016, I will have been retired from pastoring for two years. In my travels, and visiting about 60 churches, I think the number one need is EVANGELISM, REACHING THE LOST, and REVIVAL. The churches that I have visited are sound in Acts 2:38 and the One God message, along with holiness within, holiness without and separation from the world. We want to hold to those truths, but we must, again, I say we must do what Jesus asked us to do and that is, to reach the lost. This book is very inspirational concerning EVANGELISM. It needs to be read by every pastor, evangelist and saint. This is the mind of Christ.

Yours for revival and evangelism,
Elder Vaughn Morton

About the Author:

Pastor R. D. Frazier is one of the most passionate men that I have ever met concerning revival and soul winning. He is one of the premier preachers of modern Pentecost, and yet he is one of the most humble men that I know.

This book, The Purpose of the Church will be a blessing to you, but will also challenge you to do more for God. It will revive within you a burden for the lost, and incite a desire to be about the Father's business.

It will bring us back in focus as to what The Purpose of the Church really is.

I am proud to call Elder Frazier my friend.

- Pastor Randall Bowling

Part One:
Dealing with the "Question"

What is The Purpose of the Church? This question, no doubt, evokes a plethora of responses in which there would not be enough books in the land to contain them. Most answers are based on personal insight, needs, and current social enigmas. That which is most important stands within the question, "What or how does God feel and think, what was His Scriptural directive to us as the church? This being said, let us dive into the Scripture and the clarion command to the church to *"go… teach… and baptize…"*

*"**Go ye therefore, and teach** all nations, **baptizing them** in the name of the Father, and of the Son, and of the Holy Ghost: Teaching them to observe all things whatsoever I have commanded you: and, lo, I am with you*

alway, even unto the end of the world. Amen."
Matthew 28:19-20

*"And he said unto them, **Go ye** into all the world, and*
***preach the gospel** to every creature." Mark 16:15*

Naysayers believe that this command was just intended for the disciples, but this writer whole-heartedly matriculates to the college of Timothy:

"All scripture is given by inspiration of God, and is profitable for doctrine, for reproof, for correction, for instruction in righteousness:" 2 Timothy 3:16

It is not only profitable for doctrine, reproof and correction but *"instruction in righteousness."* This Scripture was written to whoever would read its pages.

We need to understand that there was a command

given here to the entire church, yea even unto every generation that would read these holy words as not only instruction, but as a command. The command is *"preach the gospel to every creature."* **The gospel**, is the *Good News.*

The *Good News* is that you do not have to be lost; you do not have to go to hell.

The *Good News* is you do not have to remain alone and destitute without God in this world.

The *Good News* is no matter what your family is like you are not bound to be just like them.

The *Good News* is that no matter what you have done, there is hope for you.

The *Good News* is no matter what you are bound by, Jesus Christ can set you free.

I am amazed at how anyone would think that this *Good News* was confined to just a few people. This gospel, He said in Mark chapter 16, verse 5, should be preached to every creature, Even we, today, are to take *this gospel* to every creature. What a mission that was given to us! What an immense responsibility to take *this gospel* and to preach it to every creature.

I am astonished how we have drifted from this original goal, and have been distracted while we walk along this gospel road. Some may say there is no way for anyone to go to the whole world. But what is wrong with reaching those that are within our proximity in our own world, in our neighborhoods, our cities, and our family and friends? The *Good News, the Gospel* is **Acts 2:38**. It is the only message that completely delivers, sets men free and places the Holy Ghost inside of them to lead and guide them into all truth.

What a Message! The devil knows this and he cannot combat it, neither has he the power capable of diminishing the splendor of *The Gospel*. Although he has not been successful in two millenniums with false doctrine and oppressions, he has not given up! Though he cannot get us away from the truth, he has a plan to delude or distract us to a point that we are not spreading the truth to anyone else. Because he knows that if he can confine and sequester *The Truth* in us by intoxicating us, who are the spokesmen that God has sent, by entangling us with life's cares, then he has accomplished the same thing as defeating it. The power of *The Gospel* was not intended to be hidden underneath a bushel.

"Let your light so shine before men, that they may see your good works, and glorify your Father which is in heaven."
Matthew 5:16

At what point are we relieved of the command and or responsibility of, *"Go Preach the Gospel"* to every creature?" What would discharge us from going and preaching? Family obligations? Could it be social obligations? Career obligations? What would it be? Is it ever acceptable in a church for saints to accumulate enough seniority that this clarion call to the lost is no longer applicable?   At what point is evangelism and Outreach no longer the main thing in a church or in your life?

Matthew chapter 4 verses 17 through 19 brings in quite a perspective of the gospel. From that time Jesus began to preach and just say, *"Repent:* for the kingdom of heaven is at hand." Again he reached out. "Jesus, walking by the sea of Galilee saw two brethren, Simon called Peter, and Andrew his brother, casting a net into the sea: for they were fishers. And he said unto them, 'Follow me, and *I will make you fishers of men.'"*

The goal and mindset of Jesus from the beginning

was propagation of the Gospel, beginning at the wedding of Canaan to the hand-picking of his disciples. He gave no promises of earthly riches, fame and fortune, In fact, a life of sacrifice and hardship was to be their earthly reward. Yet, He did give them the promise of eternal life with Him.

Evangelism and Outreach are zenith to the New Testament Church. There is no greater calling within the church than that of spreading this wonderful Gospel. How can we even think that we can face Jesus on that day, if we have hidden this priceless treasure and talent? To do so, is contradictive of the very premise for which The Gospel was given. What an ultimate greed unparalleled by anything the enemy could deliver! And right out from our own rank and file. The church should never leave this mindset and ignore the command set by the Captain of our Salvation Himself.

Can we then control the pressures of the demands

that are placed upon the church today? The social demands of every generation can absolutely feel daunting and overwhelming. The problem is when people in the pew start demanding certain accommodations to its current ills and then the pulpit begins to cave in and in all good conscience attempts to ameliorate to the cry from the pew, a cycle that begins that cannot often be stopped once it's started. Like a maelstrom, it sucks down everything that is on the surface. Somehow *the preacher and the people* must come to unity in purpose, and then fight to maintain that purpose. There is an axiom in the scripture of Hosea, "Like people, like priest." In order to maintain this unity there are some rules that will aid us in maintaining our purpose. Everything we do, speak, and build must have the lost in mind. The first sign of a dying church is when the infrastructure becomes paramount. It is detrimental when the internal programs are more important and take precedent over Outreach and evangelism. Not that infrastructure is wrong, for without it the building would fall, but most often as not, churches (i.e. organizations) tend to eventually over-emphasize and become exclusively obsessed in this area of infrastructure. For that very reason growth becomes non-existent and a perpetual maintenance program becomes paramount. An imbalance of **Outreach** versus **In-Reach** can be as damaging or damning as it's intended benefits. God desires balance. In other words, as we reach out, let us not forget that we need to accommodate the spiritual needs of those we win. To be only Outreach-focused is not what God intended for the church to be. We must not forget that saints need to be taught and disciplined. On the contrary, it is not acceptable to be so walled-in and so consumed with the mentality of *"us four and no more"* Nor is it acceptable to be so overtly consumed with a plethora of inner church programs that if put on a weighing scale with Outreach, it would propel them like a catapult.

As a church, we must never, never forget what got us where we are! Those early years of struggle, fighting and scraping for any soul that would even give us the time of day. No one was exempt from our invites, Bible studies and witnessing. Do you remember when every service was a battle to reach a certain spiritual crescendo? If someone even remotely acted like God was touching them we with supernatural speed, were immediately at their side. During worship, if one person didn't clap it caused the rest to look and wonder what happened. Beautiful and desperate were those early years. Have you given thought that they may contain the missing ingredient of growth? Because now you're busy, busy with appointments and programs. Training, teaching and guiding has consumed your time. Not to mention the family obligations and endless parties. When you first came to Christ you were possibly the only one in your family, or at least it was just you and your spouse. But now, oh how busy we are with programs, positions, appointments and family until you just don't have time for Outreach. Then the church begins what is, in most cases, an irreversible decline or attrition. If only we could remember, if only we could hear that distant faint cry of the lost. Alas, it is drowned out by the noise of today, the sounds of right now and the church or more correctly put, our local assembly begins to die. Even now as you read, some churches will have declined further than others, some will just be starting to feel ill, while others will be in the final death-throes and all you hear now is the death rattle.

Not only are churches subject to dying, but on a greater scale, most organizations and even nations are subject to death. Like gravity it affects the secular and spiritual, earthly and heavenly. The very law of the sower shows a minimum of 75% loss, the turnover is astounding! The parable as stated is definitely alarming as far as the numbers of who stays and who leaves. In all honesty, today's church is not all that different. You have to go through many to retain few. If you look up at the rear view mirror of the past and start counting those that are still in church after ten or twenty years, it can almost be depressing and lonely. We must remember then, with these apparent calculations both scriptural and real, that if we are not growing, we are dying. To become distracted in anyway, shape or form from adding to the church is a death sentence on that local assembly. In order to survive until Jesus comes, we must become committed to balance, both an inward growth and an outward growth. We must break the trend before it becomes irreversible!

Attrition to a population will eventually wipe out a culture if not corrected. Once a culture reaches a certain point there is no return, according to an article. That is when a culture's population reaches below a 3.1 child per family ratio to that of death rate, they are at risk of eventual extinction. The article noted that the Europeans, in the British Empire and France, are at an irreversible decline due to the tremendous immigration of Middle Easterners. While these countries are themselves at a ratio of 1.8 children per family, the immigrants from the Middle East are having 8.1-8.3 ratios of children. At the date of the article, February 2015, they claim the trend is now irreversible. They now have a strangle hold, not only in population, but also in electable politics and are imposing their Middle Eastern laws and culture on the European people and governments. This, as the article has stated, has now reached an almost, but not quite, state of affairs here in the United States. Because currently, as far as the Judean/Christian type churches, we are having children at a ratio of 2.8, below the needed sustainable number of 3.1, while the newly arrived Muslims are having an 8.1 ratios. *No doubt we are in a cultural decline.*

My point being far from political is, that *the point of no return* for our church is not far off if we don't wake ourselves from this slumber! Attrition, due to spiritual death and sheep swapping, which may be one in the same, will eventually decimate the numbers of our local congregation unless drastic measures are taken. In order to survive, we need to be providing for spiritual birth at a much higher rate than we currently are or suffer the extinction of the local congregation here.

Part Two:

Three Principles That Need To Be Applied If We Are To Survive.

W e find here in the scripture **(Luke 14:16-23)** these principles offered to us:

"Then said he unto him, A certain man made a great supper, and bade many: ¹⁷And sent his servant at supper time to say to them that were bidden, Come; for all things are now ready. ¹⁸And they all with one consent began to make excuse. The first said unto him, I have bought a piece of ground, and I must needs go and see it: I pray thee have me excused. ¹⁹And another said, I have bought five yoke of oxen, and I go to prove them: I pray thee have me excused. ²⁰And another said, I have married a wife, and therefore I cannot come. ²¹So that servant came, and showed his lord these things. Then the master of the house being angry said to his servant, Go out quickly into the streets and lanes of

the city, and bring in hither the poor, and the maimed, and the halt, and the blind. [22]*And the servant said, Lord, it is done as thou hast commanded, and yet there is room.* [23]*And the lord said unto the servant, Go out into the highways and hedges, and compel them to come in, that my house may be filled.*

As with all Scripture and even parables, this writer subscribes to the thought that God never has to make up Scripture and stories, but pulls from his vast reservoir to make appropriate application.

He states in verse 16, "*A certain man made a great supper,*" and I believe that there was a certain man. With that said, this certain man made this great supper and bade or invited many. He even said, "*All things are ready,*" which is indicative that the Kingdom of God is at hand, and ready for the New Testament dispensation. As mentioned in the other scriptures, the Gospel supper was rejected by those for whom were the first intended. As we have read,

"They all with one consent began to make excuse." I find it somewhat disturbing and humorously typical that the excuses are current for any generation, mainly because they are typical of human nature that never changes regardless of age or dispensation. Notice that the scripture decidedly chose the term or word, "excuse," or "make excuse." The first of them had just purchased some real estate; I find humorous. Really, who would purchase real estate without seeing it first? It is quite laughable, to say the least, and a flimsy excuse at best. Take note that I'm sure that it wasn't God's intention to display plausible excuses, as it was to show us they were in fact just excuses. What's your excuse? The second was as laughable as the first. He bought some oxen and needed to prove them. Really? Then the third, which is lamest of all, was a man who at least stated the truth without excuse, just plainly stated "I have married a wife," end of story, "I can't come!"

Now Luke describes the stories' main character, the Master, as being angry. Regardless of excuse, this caused the Master to be angry. I am at this point reminded of a couple of Scriptures that say *"Seek him while he may be found,"* and *"Today is the day of salvation."* In other words, we as mere mortals need to respond when the Master makes an invite.

We need to take careful note at this point. There were two different categories of individuals to which the Master sent an invitation. The first being the group so named as "the streets and lanes of the city" and at this point it is stated in the scripture that it was performed and yet there was room. Then the Master sent invitations to the second category, which was the "highways and hedges." This was done, and then the astounding words were declared, "That My house may be filled."

This leads to three principles:

1. It Is The Will Of God That His House Be Filled.
2. Go To People Whom Will Come.
3. The Miracle Principle.

1. IT IS THE WILL OF GOD FOR HIS HOUSE TO BE FILLED

This first principle dictates that it was and is the will of God that His house be filled, wherever that may be. If you have a house or building, it is His will that it be filled! Why would He expect otherwise? Don't let doubt obscure the potential of God. Be not deceived it's not *your potential,* but His! Keep this perspective and you will remain safe. God is not leaving the success entirely on us as men, but only desires that we do what is possible and leave the impossible to Him! The possible versus the impossible! The intention of God is that we bring them then God feeds them. God never intended that we become super-human equipped with super-talents and abilities. He's really looking more for availability than ability! Willingness is far more valuable than your money and great potential. Really potential is nothing more than one's false sense of security. This type of person really never does anything but sit around smugly critiquing those who struggle in the attempts. This reminds me of a quote I once read about football. "Football is a game where there are 22 men battling for preeminence and are in tremendous need of rest while the crowd screams advice and are in need of the exercise." Such is Outreach and church building. Just because a man is a great speaker doesn't make him the authority on building a church. Because he can move the masses doesn't qualify him in advice and mentoring. Beware! Success is more than a powerful vocabulary and presence. If I'm going to buy a house, I go to a realtor not a chef; if I need financial advice I go to a financial advisor who is qualified, not Joe-the-plumber. If I need open-heart surgery, I go to the best heart surgeon not a chiropractor. Not that the contrasted opposites mentioned aren't good in their respective fields, but the switch could be devastating. Because a man is great in one area doesn't mean he'll be equally as great in every other field. That is why God has implemented the five-fold ministry and no single minister has all five fingers regardless of what he claims.

Be it understood that the writer holds to the deep conviction that a full house is NOT negotiable with God. Why else would he improvise the Church and the Gospel of Jesus Christ? At what point in the Scripture does it instruct us to close-up shop and just wait for His return? A full house must be the drive of every church and pastor, lest we die off from attrition.

2. GO TO PEOPLE WHO WILL COME

"*From that time Jesus began to preach, and to say, Repent: for the kingdom of heaven is at hand. [18]And Jesus, walking by the sea of Galilee, saw two brethren, Simon called Peter, and Andrew his brother, casting a net into the sea: for they were fishers. [19]And he saith unto them, Follow me, and **I will make you fishers of men.**"* Matthew 4:17-19

Within principle two, there are two sub-principles that are very important:

a. If you're going to fish, go where there are fish

b. If they're not biting, go where they are biting

~

a. *If you're going to fish, go where there are fish*

So, if you're going to fish, then it only makes sense to

go where there are fish! Why go fishing in a swimming pool? We need to become Fishermen. A fisher of men; the fisher of souls. This is the intent of God and the Gospel. It may be cleaner and more aesthetically pleasant to sit by a pool and spend time, but you're never going to catch fish there. It only looks good. Much like a lot of churches and the mindset they fall into, they don't want to get dirty and rather desire to have a pleasant, clean time than a profitable one. If all else fails they may go buy themselves some fish at the market. Lord knows, that in today's world there are now markets for the souls of men. Rather than catch them yourself, you just bid to the highest for fish that someone else has gone to the trouble of catching. Unfortunately, the best fishing holes are not in picturesque, temperature-controlled settings. As one Elder told another preacher many years ago when he was showing off the beautiful forests and lakes of where he had recently settled to start a church, he said, "Brother, you can't save nature." And I say again, knowingly redundant, if you're going to fish, go where there are fish!

"And into whatsoever city or town ye shall enter, inquire who in it is worthy; and there abide till ye go thence. 12And when ye come into an house, salute it. 13And if the house be worthy, let your peace come upon it: but if it be not worthy, let your peace return to you. 14And whosoever shall not receive you, nor hear your words, when ye depart out of that house or city, shake off the dust of your feet."
Matthew 10:11-14

~

b.　　If they're not biting, go where they are biting.

"But into whatsoever city ye enter, and they receive you not, go your ways out into the streets of the same, and say, 11Even the very dust of your city, which cleaveth on us, we

do wipe off against you: notwithstanding be ye sure of this, that the kingdom of God is come nigh unto you." Luke 10:10-11

There comes a time when you need to determine that either they're biting or not. *If they're not biting, go where they are biting.* More often than not, too much time is spent in pursuing the pink elephant. Trying to catch that *good 'en,* that homeowner, business owner or well to do person. These always seem just out of our reach. They play and toy with the bait and then they are gone. Some spend such an inordinate amounts of time they often have little left for the undesirables. The problem that most seem to struggle with is the fact that the middle-class and upwards often do not have the time nor interest in God or the church unless they see an advantage for themselves. Often they are so busy carting their children to all the soccer and sport games and working two to three jobs to buy all the accouterments of a well-bred middle-class they have absolutely no time for God or a church. If we were to take an honest overall poll of most churches started from scratch in the last fifty years, we would find that they were initially started with the poor and uneducated. We have become delusional with our current wealth and upper education of today that we've convinced ourselves we now can reach the better off, or at least the working class homeowner. Not to say that they cannot be reached, but most solid, ethically built churches were not started with the upper crust. Unfortunately, to the embarrassment of many generationally Apostolic they cringe at the very thought, methinks that though time has rolled on and with technological revolution at hand, men as creatures really have not changed. I really believe that the basic fundamentals of fishing have not changed. You still have to fish where there are fish and you can only catch fish where they are biting. Too much time has been spent on seminars, programs, workshops and powerful speakers. When upon investigation you find that rather than having been pioneers in this field or participants they were really only facilitators, purveyors and gatherers of others experiences and expertise. You see everybody wants fish, it's just that it's too much effort for some, so they head to the "fish market" instead of catching their own, because it's much easier to buy fish than catch a fish. I believe that God wants soul winners not "soul shoppers." So, you've got to decide: Do you want to catch fish, or buy fish? If you're going to be a fisherman then you must adjust your techniques to continue to catch fish. But never forget that the basics are tried and true. Really it's the down-and-outers and poor that is the hungriest and most likely to be won by the gospel.

Please do not forget, after the Master had invited the privileged, and they excused their way out, He turned to those that were less fortunate yea, the poor and the destitute, those that most would consider undesirable.

I remember once when pushing a very settled congregation on reaching out to the lost, that during a service, a long-haired, somewhat disheveled man, came and sat on a pew. I watched as horrified mothers grabbed their children and purses, left the pew and fled to safer ground. Astounding how in just a few short years, they had forgotten where they came from. I wonder how God felt? In my experience when knocking doors on visitation that the middle class and upward were, to say the least, very unfriendly and acted like they were extremely inconvenienced that you knocked at their door. Whereas the poorer neighborhoods and apartment complexes where the welfare, and drug addicts live, are extremely friendly, even inviting you into their homes. Again, why go fish where they're not biting?

The problem is that everyone wants to start at the top. The Purpose of the Church wasn't meant to play a trading game with other churches. I believe that The Purpose of the church was to reach the lost, those that are in darkness. Again, we can't afford to become distracted from The Purpose!

One Sunday service, several years ago, during a Sunday school contest, Brother Sherry brought in a couple of homeless men that he had found under an overpass. They looked deplorable and smelled awful. (I even gave it a thought that I'd deduct points from his team for these *smile). But somewhere during the service while the Holy Ghost was moving one of those men, was standing with his hands in the air repenting! Lo and behold, he received the Holy Ghost speaking in other tongues. "Wow" would be an understatement; he looked and was dressed horribly. He had long greasy hair down to his shoulders, a filthy beard, a long grimy trench coat, literally the epitome of an outcast. I wasn't completely convinced that this would be a keeper. We, with much consternation and apprehension, baptized him. Needless to say, the congregation was wary, as many had at the beginning of the service distanced themselves as far as away as they could possibly get. Now, the waters of baptism were not only troubled, but also dirty. Really, to be honest, I had thought at first I would never probably see this man again, and I wasn't completely wrong. The next Wednesday night as we starting song service I noticed a visitor with Brother Sherry, which really wasn't unusual for him, as he was fearless and unrelenting in inviting, hauling, yea, dragging new people to church. This man visiting had a hugely oversized white shirt on with a tie and the points on the collar met in the middle. I went down from the platform to ask Brother Sherry who this visitor was and meet the man. To my amazement this was the same man from Sunday night, and yet it wasn't. This man wasn't only in a white shirt and tie, but had a haircut and shave, completely unrecognizable from the man on Sunday. He was incidentally wearing one of Brother Sherry's shirts and tie, Brother Sherry was 6'4 and this man, was about 5'8. He said that his name was John Paul, and he lived in a shack by the freeway behind Stater Bros grocery store. This man was used by God to ignite a revival that would eventually add to our church upwards to a hundred people in the next few years. I've never seen a new convert - convert so rapidly. He would come by the church during the day and ask to work, clean or whatever his hand found to do. A great-natured man, he was with a fervent zeal to learn and do all that he could for the kingdom of God. He never missed a service until many weeks had passed and suddenly he wasn't there? I didn't think much of it until two or three services had passed and he wasn't there. And really, I thought that as with many that come in from drugs and tremendous degradation that possibly he slipped back. Then suddenly, there he was in service again, yet from the distance on the platform I could tell something was wrong. When I went back to where he was sitting I saw that he was badly bruised and cut up with black and blue bruises, and swollen split lips. It was obvious that he had been severely beaten, and became evident as we spoke. Evidently he'd been witnessing to two or three others who share his shack, but they became violent. Such is sometimes the case with the very destitute of drug addicts; they are often not only drugged out of their minds, but are demon possessed. We prayed with him and were trying to get him away from those miscreants, yet he was adamant that he stay a while longer to keep witnessing. After he was healing up quite well, he'd be fast to his feet during testimony service to give God glory. Man, he really could testify! I thought if he kept that up, God after would call him up to preach. While testifying, he in less than three minutes, would have the entire church on their feet. This man had a gift to speak and God, through him, was changing the entire fabric of the church. Excitement was in the air every service as often happens when new souls come. Then after several weeks had passed, suddenly John Paul wasn't there and I was leaving to preach a meeting. I hadn't had time to inquire before I had left, but thought Brother Sherry would keep me informed, so I boarded my plane.

I was having a great time at this meeting in Middle America and enjoying the fellowship when suddenly I received a call that desperately messaged me call home. Upon doing so, I was informed that John Paul was in the hospital dying. I was totally shocked and panicked. Unfortunately after returning home, I found out I was too late, he had died. Brother Sherry brought me up to date. He said that John Paul had been doing what he did best, witnessing.

Unfortunately, it was to the same men he roomed with, but this time they, in the middle of the night had beaten him again and then poured gasoline on him and set him on fire. He died in the hospital before I could get back. To make matters worse, as we tried to locate his body for burial, they had buried him in an unmarked grave in a potter's field. There was no investigation or inquest to this heinous crime, as often the case with what society claims as homeless-undesirables. I was crushed, to say the least, mortified, that all this took place while I was away.

Church services became an explosion of revival and new souls, after the knowledge of his death. Oh, that revival fires would burn and we would not forget and lose our direction and *purpose of the Church*! Suddenly, church had begun to change, from ambivalent self-protectionists to risk-taking warriors with a purpose, needing to take vengeance against the devil. I'm convinced that there are more John Pauls out there! Oh, who will go search and find them?

One of the reasons for this message, and now this book, is to remind us lest we forget.

Already, I can see lethargy settling into the pews. It's getting more and more difficult to rally the troops. I fear, as America has forgotten for the most part, about 9/11, as our ever busy lives distract us, I'm watching a church slowly lose its perspective and focus on *The Purpose of the Church*. Families, jobs, vacations, and parties, have caused our people to become self-absorbed with our little worlds. When and while we are missing some of the greatest unsearchable riches of the New Testament, power and blessings that aren't measured by terra firma and her limits. I speak of spiritual things that the carnal are now shaking their heads in wonderment, and the slightly spiritual are faintly moved by well-wishing emotion. Oh, I hear the voice of the Lord crying faintly, somewhere echoing, from somewhere deep in the recesses of my mind and heart. He's looking and searching for a man. I can almost make out the words, "Who will go?" The cries of the lost, the hurting, the abused and the poor have reached the Master and His heart is broken. "But I'm so busy", as one after another make excuse to the master. Oh, that someone reading these amateur and inadequate lines would not only feel my heartbeat, but that of God's too. Truly, *The Purpose of the Church* will cause us to have to break out of our comfort zone.

3. THE MIRACLE PRINCIPLE

"*T*hen he which had received the one talent came and said, Lord, I knew thee that thou art an hard man, reaping where thou hast not sown, and gathering where thou hast not strawed: 25And I was afraid, and went and hid thy talent in the earth: lo, there thou hast that is thine. 26His lord answered and said unto him, Thou wicked and slothful servant, thou knewest that I reap where I sowed not, and gather where I have not strawed:" Matthew 25:24-26*

This parable, when I was starting a church some many years ago, made a tremendous impact on me. Not that I hadn't read it many times before and even preached and or taught it, but I now was in a tremendous strait of sorts. After having endured the first two to three beginning years of no people (I was naïve and thought that church starting was winning new souls...smile), we now had baptized and won around thirty people and had hit a snag. We had suddenly gone dry and there were no new people coming to the services for several weeks. I had been seeking God and trying to figure out what happened. Then suddenly while preaching, I made a completely bold statement, as I will explain momentarily. Now when men start claiming, "The Lord gave me this or that" I have often said, "Well you've knocked out all argument," I mean like, how do you argue with God? But really, I do believe that it was God now, even though at the time I was somewhat less than confident of that. While I was exhorting and making a plea for people to bring visitors, which we hadn't had any for several weeks, I made this very bold statement, "We're going to pass out 2,000 flyers Saturday and then on Sunday we will have visitors, even though none will be from the flyers." "Wow!" I thought, "Did I just say that?" At this point I thought, I'll either end up a false prophet with no credibility or I will be giving God glory on Sunday. I

THE PURPOSE OF THE CHURCH

then began to further expostulate and actually felt anointed while I went on. I said that the parable of the talent in Matthew the wicked servant claimed that the Lord was a hard man (in Luke he said "austere man") one that was so proficient that he said, *"Reaped where he had not sown and gathered where he hadn't strawed."* So I began to preach to our small congregation that because God has a law that He Himself states that through the writer that *no flesh shall glory*, and so that would mean, that no one tool of man in Outreach should ever receive the glory, else we then would end up commercializing the tool over *the God of the tool.* (It does seem that as men, we are often, not given to this sort of thing. As men, we like that which we can touch and feel, rather than the spiritual, this tends to be a faith-thing.) I went on to say, that evidently this wicked servant's problem wasn't lying, but a faith-thing and plain laziness. The Lord then said, in essence, *"Yes, I do reap where I have not sowed, and gather where I have not strawed!"* There is a law here being spoken. I am using this as my "miracle principle": the Lord reaps and gathers everywhere. What He wants is for His servants to just do something, anything, but don't just sit there idle. It is He that adds daily to the church, not us . We're to just do and be available to the work and He'll add daily to the church daily such as should be saved. What He doesn't want is an idle church or people. If he allowed any one certain tool to be the answer then men would put it on paper and start doing seminars and conferences and write books so that all would have a guaranteed success. (Oh wait, that's exactly what many have already done.) Also many have found what works for one and in one part of the country doesn't always work here.

Because of this law of reaping and gathering, after Saturday's visitation and passing out the 2,000 flyers, we will have visitors even though we haven't had any for weeks! none of them will be from the flyers.

THE PURPOSE OF THE CHURCH 47

It was because God wants to prove to us His mighty power and that if we'll do the possible, He'll do the impossible. After having made these bold proclamations, after the service, my faith began to wane, to say the least. I told my wife I was worried because this could have caused us to retreat and lose all that we've accomplished so far. So we had the flyers made and passed them out on Saturday. Come Sunday morning I was sweating bullets. I went early enough as to beat everybody to church by hours. I thought I could try and pray my way through this possible catastrophe and maybe God would have mercy on me because of much prayer. Hey, who knows? The music was starting as my wife began to play and I slowly started to lift my head up with great trepidation and dread. As I looked around the church, there wasn't one visitor but 15-20 visitors! I was overwhelmed, to say the least. Then for the final test, after the song service, as what would become my habit, I would greet the visitors and then I plug ahead and asked the dreaded question, ugh, *"How many today came from having received a flyer?"* and to my amazement, not one hand went up! The church was astounded, as was I. It was not a time to gain praise for my expert prophecy and know-how, but rather we gave God the glory, as we only did the possible and God did the impossible. This taught me a lesson that I would never forget: The miracle principle really in a nutshell is that we need to get busy and just do something! When we become lazy and preoccupied with life we tend to forget the challenging thrill of beholding God doing His miraculous work and power.

This brings me to a favorite quote by Theodore Roosevelt:

"It is not the critic who counts; not the man who points out how the strong man stumbles, or where the doer of deeds could have done them better. The credit belongs to

the man who is actually in the arena, whose face is marred by dust and sweat and blood; who strives valiantly; who errs, who comes short again and again, because there is no effort without error and shortcoming; but who does actually strive to do the deeds; who knows great enthusiasms, the great devotions; who spends himself in a worthy cause; who at the best knows in the end the triumph of high achievement, and who at the worst, if he fails, at least fails while daring greatly, so that his place shall never be with those cold and timid souls who neither know victory nor defeat."

If we are to have revival and maintain *The Purpose of the Church*, we cannot afford to be beguiled by distractions; which is seemingly the easy road to success. The miracle principle is doing whatever you find your hand to do. There is not one tool that exceeds all others, but, **"Just do something"**: from knocking doors, to home Bible studies, candy rains to free donuts. It really doesn't matter what you do as long as it's legal and moral. Many men these days having the luxury of having never worked, nor having to scrape, fight and struggle. They sit smugly in their lofty inherited seats of preeminence and popularity. They are surrounded by their personalized sycophants of yes-men, while dictating to others unbelievable demands, while they themselves will not lift a finger. They speak of their revelatory dictates of what God will bring into their churches if He wants to. They seem to believe their only duty is to study new and more fantastic messages to their stagnated numbers. Forgetting that we are the hands, feet and mouth of the Master. Never forget that! If we were not meant to be His vehicles then there would be no need for men. When you're starting a church from nothing things can get pretty desperate, especially when no one supports you other than your own two hands and God. Coming into an empty building, night after night, can be both sobering and revelatory. A man's measure and convictions are really never known by himself or others until he starts pastoring or starts a church. It's then, under the pressure and fire, he discovers himself. An empty storefront or building does not constitute a church; it's the people that constitute a church. So don't be too haughty on an empty building, your reverence is imaginary and quixotic at best. If you don't get busy, it'll remain a figment of your imagination and dreams. In other words, don't get too religious too soon! Yes, I must confess that I've used the same building as a place for Bible Study, then broke it down rearranged it a little and served donuts, cake and coffee. Aghast are you? Yes, I'm guilty of being somewhat ambivalently acrimonious of the sacrosanct. My error, I was desperate, there was no one waiting to hand me a ready-made congregation. Again, the miracle principle is, "Just do something" when you do what is possible for you, God will do the impossible!

As a church, we cannot afford to become complacent and or distracted. Oh, that somebody would break out of the traces and out of the box! There really is a world that is lost and on the way to hell. There really are still people out there that are soaking their pillows with tears of despair wondering if there could possibly be help for them? And many still wondering, where are the real churches with real people and real pastors? I realize we are but human, but I wonder how does God feel?

Does He weep when the cries of all the lost come before Him? The hurt and pain of the abused and beaten as they whimper and sob? Are we now so insulated in the comforts of His blessings and goodness that their cries are now muffled to our ears? I know, you've already done your part years ago and you may feel it's time for the younger generation to do something. I guess you're retired. I'm so glad that not everybody feels that way.

A man who recently died in Brazil who I was blessed to know as Pastor Gilmar Rodrigues Machado, came to the Lord as a middle-aged homeless man. He was such a severe desperate alcoholic that he would steal ethanol gas for its alcohol content and drink it. Yet because somebody wasn't particular regarding the status of people they witnessed to, they preached to him the gospel!

Pastor Gilmar Machado   11/24/1955 ~ 04/29/2014

He later became an unbelievable preacher and witness, there was no place too dangerous or off limits to Gilmar; he was fearless and always up in the front worshipping, at every special meeting, when I was there in Brazil. Even when others were seated in places of distinction and honor, Gilmar was there in the front with his rag for sweat, jumping and running while he was worshipping. Then when the preaching started it was like he was super-charged and would follow me throughout the entire building while I preached screaming his "Amen" and exultations. When the altar service began he was one of the first there on his face weeping. Never have I met many his equal in dedication and zeal. I guess the scripture is true, *"Wherefore I say unto thee, her sins, which are many, are forgiven; for she loved much: but to whom little is forgiven, the same loveth little."* No wonder so many sit resolutely content in their gilded cages, of un-thankfulness.

Finally, my prayer and hope is, "Lord please don't let me lose sight of my direction and vision of *The Purpose of the Church*. Soul winning is not an elective course in church school or a time-limited indentured servitude. It has no expiration, only we do. There is no discharge in this warfare!

Thank you for reading!
Eld. R. D. Frazier

Made in the USA
Columbia, SC
18 June 2024

37254438R00033